Wendy Lee IrWIN

INNERKNOWLEDGE

Root's & Rock's

Because every mind, body & spirit
deserves a little R&R

Gotham Books

30 N Gould St.
Ste. 20820, Sheridan, WY 82801
https://gothambooksinc.com/

Phone: 1 (307) 464-7800

Published by Gotham Books (June 9, 2023)

ISBN: 979-8-88775-316-4 (H)
ISBN: 979-8-88775-314-0 (P)
ISBN: 979-8-88775-315-7 (E)

Because of the dynamic nature of the Internet, any web addresses or links contained in this book may have changed since publication and may no longer be valid.

The views expressed in this work are solely those of the author and do not necessarily reflect the views of the publisher, and the publisher hereby disclaims any responsibility for them.

CONTENTS

Root's & Rock's 1

Hot and Cold 100 7

Degrees Apart 7

Ego Food and Ego Posion and Your Psyche 11

Chakras 55

Chakra Chart 59

Restore; Renew; Revitalize; 63

Let's Rock and Roll! 64

ROOT'S & ROCK'S

your spiritual guide to your personal power because every Body, Mind and Spirit deserves a little R and R.

These written statements have not been evaluated by the Food & Drug Administration; Furthermore, this is not intended to treat, cure, diagnose, heal anybody or replace doctor recommended medicine or medical advice. Seek the attention of a qualified physician or practitioner before using this book.

Living Root's and Rock's and their healing properties;
I have found to be a wonderful source of getting the Mind, Body and Spirit in balance.

Utilizing Root's are a source of herbal recipes, some say there is not enough scientific evidence to determine if any of the herbal recipes are a cure, that aid or prevents a stronger, healthier and spiritual side of life. Herbs listed here may be bought in an herbal store and taken as recommended by the seller.

Utilizing Rock's to their full benefit placing the gemstones on the body most medical doctors say gems healing has no evidence found that the gemstones have any effect on the body, oh well they don't have to use my book.

My studies show, each kind of Gem-Stone has its natural chemical combination. Now supplied easy to view and absorb, this information about gem-stones listed here in that may be bought by that distribution and used as a touch stone or worn as jewelry to receive optimal benefits.

First, I want to thank God for supplying me the tools that I needed to accomplish this book and in everything I do. Also providing me with my angel, guiding me on this path of: Herbal Teas A.K.A. "Tisanes"; French pronunciation "Ti-Zan" Zodiac Signs; Gem-Stone properties; Charkas Points, knowledge that paves my path of wisdom, that I am now able to share with you, here in this book. I have found some fascinating studies over a period of seven years, now available for you, in this publication, here for your personalized connections;

When working with Gem-Stones, Zodiac signs, Herbs and Charkas points, linking them together and formulating recipes that I have formulated for each of the 12 Zodiac signs; I use this particular path for my own spiritual growth as well as the many clients of mine, throughout the decade they have given testimonies statements, that it creates a better stronger Mind, Body, and Spirit; In-so-much.

I look forward to hearing the results, you have discovered through your personal connection with this formula provided herein; Enjoy using these wonderful recipes that I am very Joyful to bring forth;

I am so grateful!

The planets are singing and each one had its own musical note, that is connected to our life path, pertaining to the zodiac signs, planets, charka points, minerals it releases, and the physical body parts; Here are the musical notes; mineral; body part; and the healing properties the planets emanate when orbiting;

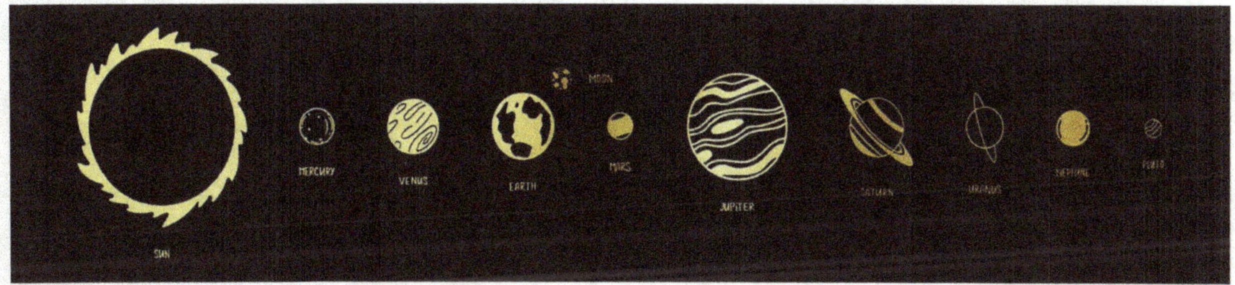

Sun (F) in Leo F is the note calcium is the mineral; Body part is muscles and the heart.

Mercury (C sharp) in Gemini it is D sharp is the note for potassium the mineral; Body parts are the arms, circulatory system, and the throat.

Mercury (C sharp) in Virgo is C sharp is the note for selenium the mineral; Body part is the lower intestine.

Venus (A) in Libra is B is the note for copper the mineral; Body parts are the eye's and loans.

Venus (A) in Taurus is A is the note for iodine the mineral; Body parts are the throat, neck and eye's.

Earth (C) # selenium is the mineral; Body part fat cells pancreas and the small intestine.

Moon in Crab (A), (B) and (Ab) are the notes iodine, copper and zinc are the minerals; Body parts are the lung's and breast.

Mars (D) in Arise A is the note for iodine the mineral; Body parts are the back of the head and neck.

Mars (D) and in Scorpio D sharp for potassium C sharp is the note for selenium the minerals; Body parts are the loans and lower intestine.

Jupiter (F) sharp and in Sagittarius (G) is the note for manganese, zinc and chromium are the minerals; Body parts are bladder and hips.

Saturn (D) is for iron in Capricorn is the note D sharp is potassium the mineral; Body parts are the knees and joints.

Saturn (D) in Aquarius G sharp and D sharp is the notes for iron magnesium and potassium are the minerals; Body parts are the leg's, throat and circulatory system.

Uranus (G) sharp in Aquarius the minerals frequently found on Uranus is silicates C minor calls amino acids methane or methionine. Body parts are shins, calves, ankles. The methane makes Uranus blue.

Neptune (G) sharp is the note for magnesium is the mineral; Body parts are the feet and liver.

Pluto (C) sharp in Scorpio (D) is the note for Iron C sharp is for selenium and G sharp is for magnesium are the minerals; Body parts are circulatory system, genitals and lower intestines.

Connecting with your zodiac sign, patterns and energy fields.

Everyone was born in a certain season Spring, Summer, Fall, or Winter. Example: Virgo 8/24 - 9/23 The gem-stones listed here are connected with your zodiac sign, in-so-much, when the gems have reached their peak of full value, this is determined by the planetary aliment concerning the zodiac signs; Example the planet Mercury rules Virgo and Gemini but the season are different for both, the gems that are connected to the individual zodiac sign carries a different path, compound; Here in my study, I have formulated the gem-stones sought to hold the healthiest paths for your zodiac signs that may improve and create balance for your life; Connecting all 12 zodiac signs, gems, and their planets in the solar system, which are in increasing distance from the sun. starting with Mercury, Venus, Earth, Moon, Mars, Jupiter, Saturn, Uranus, Neptune. Pluto, and Charon in 2003 was discovered in our neighborhood UB313 is considered part of the system, for as a real name has not been assigned to this object as of 2006.

HOT AND COLD 100 DEGREES APART.

Facts of freezing and boiling points is exactly 100 degrees apart the boiling point is 212 degrees Fahrenheit and is 180 degrees apart the freezing point is 32 degrees Celsius is the temperature at which no heat. Daniel Gabriel Fahrenheit was a German physicist 1686-1736 he invented the mercury thermometer 1709. and "introduced the temperature scale 1714 Fahrenheit" used the body temperature to start his test. Anders Celsius was a Swedish astronomer, physicist a mathematician a professor of astronomy at university known for his scale of temperature thermometer and presented "Celsius in 1742" using the waters and air at freezing temperature to start his test. The Kelvin a British inventor and chemist used temperature points starting at absolute zero degrees K is defined all molecular movement stops; Kelvin published a paper in 1848 on an absolute thermometric scale that states in fact -273 degrees. refer to 373.15k 100 kelvin -273.15k that being said this is the gage or formula for the planets hot Fahrenheit and cold Celsius. like the "little church in your head" I created a tool that may be applied as the human temperament gage, I named "little church in your head in 2001".
"Little church in your head" - Wendy Irwin

Imagine a little church in your head this is where you gather all your information, now draw a line under neath of it, now put your fingers out in front of you about shoulders length, and slowly draw them into one another, as you reach about 7 inches apart imagine putting two vertical lines to mark a boundaries point like this ________(_______)________ in-so-much, this is your playground an even temperament so that we can understand and be understood, now for the example of extreme behavior off of the chart, far to the right is the Fahrenheit degree and is a very hot, active energy, and considered a "Hot Head" losing control of one's advantage is outside of the boundary line and in an extreme extraverted manners, and in the worst case scenario one who might attempt a murder, coin the phrase "he was so upset he saw red" At the oppose end of my scale all the way on the left, is off the chart cool, a Celsius degree a very slow energy flow, cold energy can be considered an introvert shy behavior and losing control of one's advantage is outside of the boundary line "listless" and in extreme cases the worse scenario, one

who might attempt a suicide. to coin this phrase "he was so depressed". I will be publishing this study on how to balance dynamics using my targeted discovery How to use the Chakras chart; gemstones, singing bowls, and a total feng-shui for the mind, body, and spirit, created for optimal results.

A full tutorial of Chakra charts also of the Bagua or Pa Kua, the nine sides of Gua Understanding best use of yin and yang to enlighten you physical and emotional house paying attention to our bodies health, proper energy, oxygen for cells, and wellbeing respectfully, creating a list of fresh fruits, and vegetables that brings optimal balance through your zodiac sign for you, in-so-much; This is your birthright not a privilege; And more on using method in my forthcoming publications; Next Wendy's Whimsical Recipes coming soon!

Available today! created for you, Wendy's miracle herbal salts, spiritual magic in a bottle! yes, they are bath salts, designed to execute your intention quicker; Formulated with sound production Wendy playing the Tibetan singing bowls, and speaking mantras that give a boost to your spiritual world, all in a bath soak, of warm water, while listening to created mantra for your particular intention, find one that serves you best; Especially created them to hone in on your desire, Enjoy!

+Whimsical Rose+

Attract affection:

+Nook of the Forest+

Eliminate past negative attachments:

+Pixies Paradise +

Brings marital peace & Happiness:

+Fruit of the Vine+

Surround yourself with Love.

iinnerknowledge makes no claim to treat, cure, anybody.

I know your body loves to heal itself; Ask; Seek; Knock; You can create bliss now, experiences your best life! Paving the way to building a better you! Then you may seek out others, if they are true to your vibration or not, when two are in agreement, your true heart produces "miracles" that manifest. (when your heart is in your desire no request is to extreme) see simple solutions for the I am.

If you're not sure what that is plause along you may pick it up by method, bring on the glow.

EGO FOOD AND EGO POSION AND YOUR PSYCHE

Those who are able to see beyond the shadows and lies of their culture will never be understood, let alone believed by the masses.

- Plato

Herein, I refer to ego food, as a positive vibrations, and ego poison, as the negative vibrations, a catch and release system of things that no longer serve you, because living in the now is building a better you not living in the high achievements of once created, nor past times of dwelling on the lesser unfortunate past events; Or thoughts of grandeur, This will hold you back and keep you from your true life mission; nevertheless we may benefit from solutions through focused thoughts, thrusting, flushing the ego poison is crucial.

A note about the qualities for your zodiac sign and the influence they play in our everyday life. I have put together groups; Insights from our solar system; Stories they tell me. yup the universe is talking! Here are the trends that create three different aspects the Beginning, the Middle, and the End; I am referring to Cardinal, Mutable, and Fixed, qualities I believe it is all in God's plan to create a perfect universe for us to call upon, for balancing groups of individuals. Managers you might want to review your employee applications to put a dynamic team together to complete your campaign with a beginning a middle and the conclusion of the events.

Cardinal signs they are the Beginners, promoters, the creates, they set the stage. Fixed Signs are the tireless worker who don't give up until the work is complete. Mutable signs are the complete picture, the idea of the finished product, they take the Beginning along with the Middle products and turn it in to the main performance.

Cardinal signs are; Aries, Cancer, Libra, Capricorn, the Cheer leaders, they start every season Ares in Spring, Cancer in Summer, Libra in Autumn, Capricorn in the Winter, these are the first set, the leaders the initiator to a great plan the Beginners of each season.

Fixed signs are; Taurus, Leo, Scorpio, Aquarius, the solid tried and true sign's because they have done the hard work; Taurus in spring, Leo in summer, Scorpio in Autumn, Aquarius in Winter, the Middles will take the value of the Cardinal and go the distance.

Mutable signs are; Gemini, Virgo, Sagittarius, Pisces, the End of each season and seer of the bigger picture, they know how to prepare a winning plan, completing the season they have seen it all, start to finish, Gemini in spring, Virgo in summer, Sagittarius in Autumn, Pisces in Winter, Mutable signs are the most flexible, versatile, the season is ripe for them to put the complete product together perfected with the midas touch.

In aliment with our planetary solar system in-so-much, is as follows, nearest to the Sun; Mercury, Venus, Earth, Moon, Mars, Jupiter, Saturn, Uranus, Neptune, Pluto, and the most distant planets is 2003 UB313, and is 97 times father from the Sun also now reference as planets 9. The Moon is about 400 times smaller than the sun but it is actually 400 times closer; When the sun orbits around the earth 365 days it takes the moon directly between the earth and the sun and that is called a solar eclipse.

Medical astrologer's have determined points of the body associated with each Zodiac Sign, that are believed to rule over the body that are likely to experience trouble with, for instance I have found and formulated, recipes for a path of each 12 Zodiac Sign's, here is my result! Example for, Pisces born 2/20-3/20 may have concerns with the feet and most likely experience swelling or aching. I have found that when Jade is recommended and used as a management plan for the gem stone healing, this brings self-awareness, helps in a harmonious energy flow that alleviates the causes and effect, in Pisces; Jade is my gem of choice, may bring Harmony to the body, wisdom for the mind, Trust for the spirit. understanding our mind, body, and spirit to building a better you. remember minds and parachutes work in a similar fashion they only work when they open. Jade is used on sixth Chakra and solar plexus Chakra for energy flow. Never the less, I have found the herb Juniper berry may improve digestion and circulation as it does stimulate the kidneys, a jump starts to joint and muscle flexibility and pain relief. Harvest time is December 21st, before the frost comes, a perfect time of year we need the essential, allowing the berries to ripen, before picking, native to temperate regions of the Northern Hemisphere. The Pisces body, responds to the herb gem, allowing the current dynamic to move and release the block of energy; Now moving forward; Building a better you. Extending this example for Pisces born 2/20-3/20 that is the last day of Winter and the gem is ripened or peeked in this half months of the year and the gem is jade, native to China and Canada, where the waters are colder off the Atlantic and western Pacific Ocean for China; The jade caves are found, the components are $NaAl\ [si206] + Ca,\ Fe,\ Mg,\ Mn$ indicating a chemistry match compounds of atoms, elements structure of properties, behavior and the changes they undergo during a reaction with this staple or subject here being Pisces.

Pisces
constellation

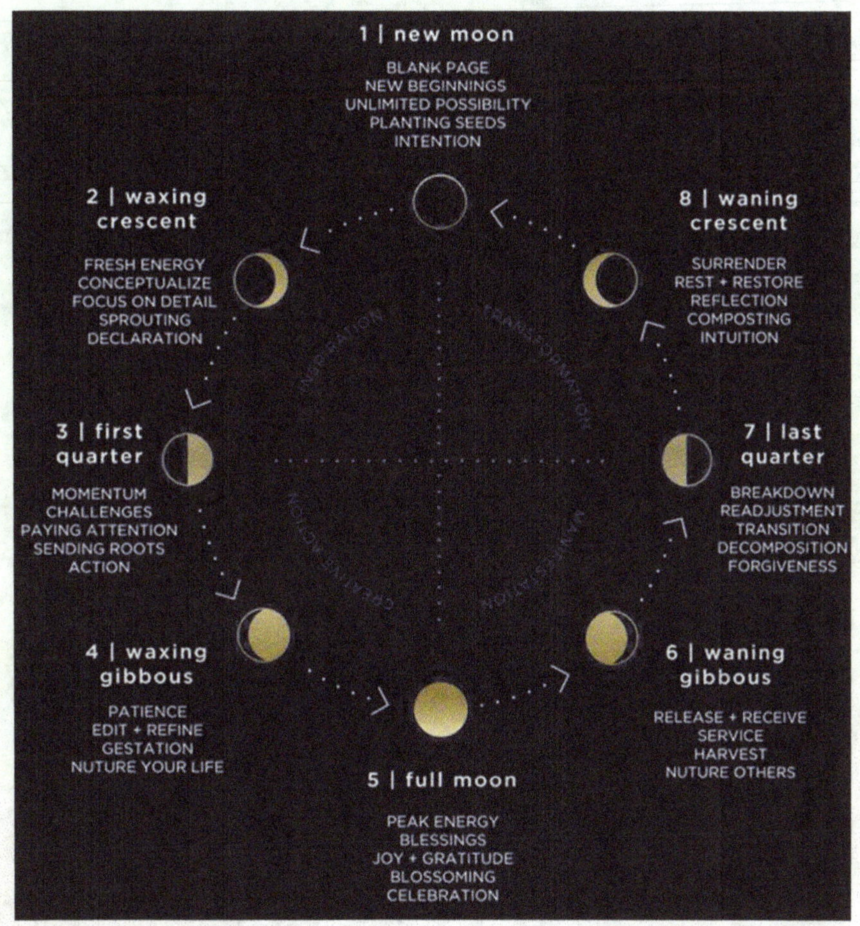

Concerning Northern Hemisphere beginning with Spring

Spring - begins with Vernal Equinox

March 19 - ends June 19- ^ am-pm.

Summer - begins with Solstice

Junes 20 - ends September 23- ^ am-pm.

Fall/Autumn - begins with Autumnal Equinox

September 22 - ends December 20- ^ am-pm.

Winter - begins with Solstice

December 21 - ends March 18 - ^ am-pm.

Each year may vary due to equinox and solstice and leap years, times that change dates, you may refer to-"the old farmer's almanac" founded in 1792. for cusp signs, I have followed through with the remaining 11 zodiac signs, and have matched them for a more personalized path, developed for you, in this publication, it is my work study, that now is available y for all who are seeking inner knowledge about ones self.

Aries: Your ruler planet is Mars, color is reddish brown. Iron is the solid, and represents male energy, the red planet is the fourth planet from the sun and the second smallest planet in the solar system after Mercury, Mars planet symbols are of desire, action, energy and survival instincts its nature is aggression, animal instincts, anger and survival skills. Known as God of war, Mars is much colder than the earth on average is about minus 80 degrees Fahrenheit and not because it is farther from the sun, it has a thinner atmosphere and does not support a strong greenhouse resilience and can get minus 60 Celsius.

Happy Birthday ARIES: 03/21 - 04/20.

Fire. symbol: Ram.

Mind concerns: Ego.

Body concerns: Head, brain, eyes, and face.

Spiritual concerns: Promote self-esteem = friends of true heart. Trust worthy people will demote a false sense of self. belief begins in you.

Aries are; Cheerful, passionate, leaders, relentless.

Aquamarine: Fifth, sixth, seventh Chakra: May reduce inflammation for this Aries with trouble spots head, brain, eyes, face.

Jasper: Solar plexus and root Chakra: You may find jasper may help in achieving harmony and peace: You may also find jasper disposes of jealousy and stimulates fertility and of sexual feelings.

Herb: Lobelia: sooth's inflamed ears, head, and nose, the soft tissues areas, it has known to aid from miscarriages, Lobelia is a shrub native to North America also known as Indian tobacco used by Cherokee, Iroquois, Penobscot tribes to cure respiratory, gnats, and heal muscle disorders.

Taurus: Your ruler planet is Venus, color is pale Yellow. copper is the solid, this is called the planet of love and represents female energy. Symbolizes Goddess of love as a result rules over love and money this planet shines the brightest, somewhat of a male influence is present, it is also the hottest in the solar system, second from the sun, although it is not the closest to the sun, the dense atmosphere holds heat creating a greenhouse similarity that heats the earth, Venus can reach 870 degrees Fahrenheit that can melt lead and can cool to 462 degrees Celsius.

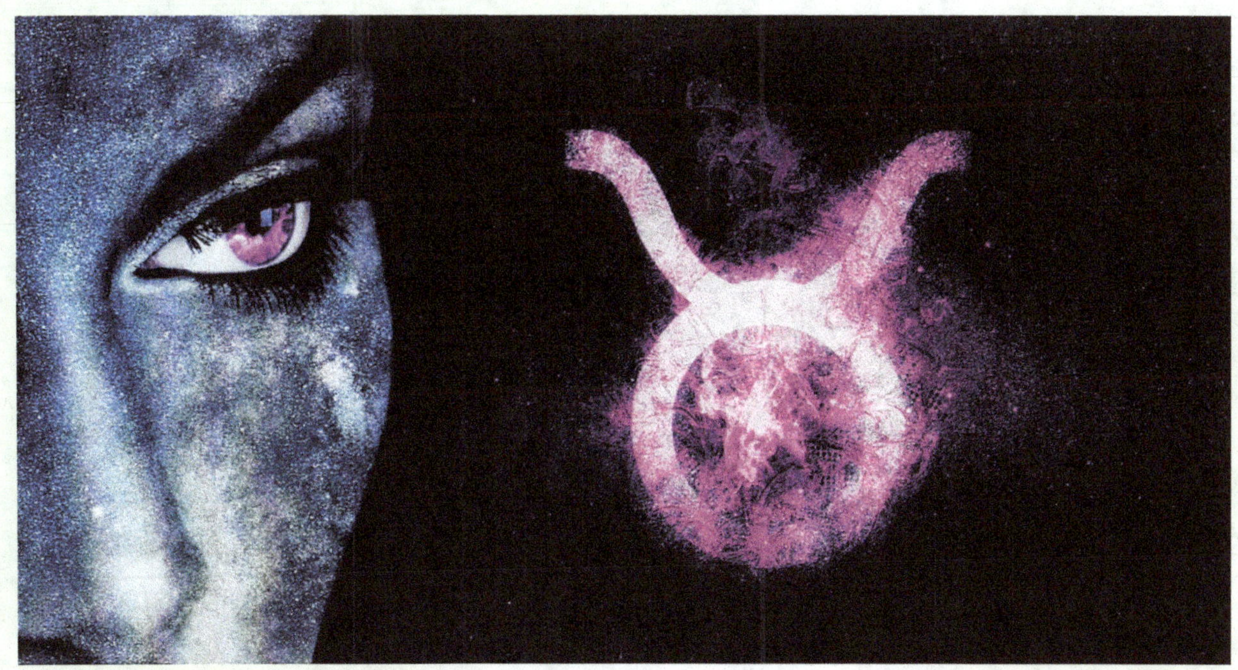

Happy Birthday TAURUS: 04/21 - 05/20.

Earth. symbol: Bull.

Mind concerns: Emotions / listening.

Body concerns: Neck, throat, ears.

Spiritual concerns: Inner peace, healing one's self in a dream state; What this Taurus mind can conceive you will achieve.

Taurus are; stubborn, famous, artistry, love luxury.

Diamond: All Chakras: Diamonds are used for career advantages. Creates new ideas and foresight for the future.

Rhodochrosite: Heart Chakra. May give a strong sense of self and emotion, broadens one's worth of financial situation and thinking.

Aventurine: Heart Chakra. a real promoter of peace and harmony to this Taurus, also gives an energy boost to that over worked Taurus. Calms and revitalize.

Goldenseal

Herb: Golden Seal: Is an antibacterial may aid in immune stimulator as it increases blood. lessens the onset of tumors combat liver problems, nose bleeds, earaches, an eye wash, for infected, or tired eyes. Found in North America Georgia, Missouri, and at times at far South as Quebec.

Gemini: Your ruler is Mercury. Color is Gray. Quick Silver is the solid and represents both female and male energy. It symbolizes the thinker, a winged cap of communication, it concerns itself with the head, a year on mercury is 88 days long, being a wind channel, this quality resonates a bit more on the feminine side, traits, a Goddess of information and knowledge; and is the smallest planet; This planet is closest to the Sun therefore reaches temperatures of 800 degrees Fahrenheit 427 degrees Celsius on average.

Happy Birthday GEMINI: 05/21 - 06/20.

Air. symbol: Twins.

Mind concerns: Over thinking.

Body concerns: Hands, lungs, nervous system.

Spiritual concerns: If you think a thing or not your right.

Over analyze common situations, take time to discover the true inner person you are, and whom you form relationships with.

Gemini's are; impulsive, indecisive, talkative, nosy, easy-going.

Amber: Navel Chakra: May bring peace and confidence, a blood warming tool for this cool temperature Gemini.

May open up new paths.

Orange sapphire is often called orange paparazzi: Sacral Chakra.

Blue sapphire on the fifth Chakra. lowers the stress of anxiety nervous, disorders; Blue sapphire brings people true of heart.

Rock Crystal: All Chakras: May clear the mind and path for spiritual stability.

Marjoram: A natural diaphoretic will promote perspiration and aid in subsiding cold and flu symptoms due to fever; May aid in sore throats and tooth aches calm and relieve nerves. Native to the Mediterranean region also found in Asia.

Cancer: Your ruler is the Moon. Color is silver. Solid is the color. it symbolizes deepest feelings and needs, being Feminine energy associated with the night and eternity, it represents the unconscious and all that is driven by the water, known as the Goddess of Selene and that the Moon controls the water in our body as well as on Earth; Waters that orbits the Earth. The Earth is the closest to the Moon, when the sun exposes itself to the Moon the temperature can reach 260 degrees Fahrenheit and when the Sun goes down temperatures can reach 127 degrees Celsius.

Happy Birthday CANCER: 06/21 - 07/22.

Water. symbol: Crab.

Mind concerns: False since of security, through emotions.

Body concerns: Breast, stomach, lungs, and female parts.

Spiritual concerns: Slow and steady forward wins the race. not sideways, loyalty starts with yourself first.

Ruby: Roots Chakra: Creates sexual energy, gives strength to the body's immune system; Rubies ward off many infections, great for all circulation. Keep heart balanced and strong.

Cancer are sensitive to their environments, intuitive, self-protective, sneaky.

Emerald: Heart Chakra: May concours mood swings as it may absorb negative energy using this gem may keep this crab protected.

Moonstone: Sacral Chakra: The best stone for crabs, as the moon is this signs planet. May aid in female parts and thyroid.

LICORICE ROOT

Licorice: Contains a natural hormone that may replace cortisone and normalizes ovulation. Popular in Europe and Asia it is found growing wild in this climate.

Leo: Your ruler is the Sun, color is Gold. Gold is the solid. The Sun is the total life force, and represents male energy symbols of indulgent and the ego of higher self, it is exalted in Aries, as both love to be the center of attention. the Sun is God of radiant known as Apollo; The Sun is the Star in the center of the solar system, that travels around it. 10,000 degrees Fahrenheit and 5,500 degrees Celsius and is, Astronomers use the Sun distance between the Earth and the Sun as a measurer meter. The Sun is the hottest planet, it is the plasma that generates a magnetic force of energy for life on our planet today.

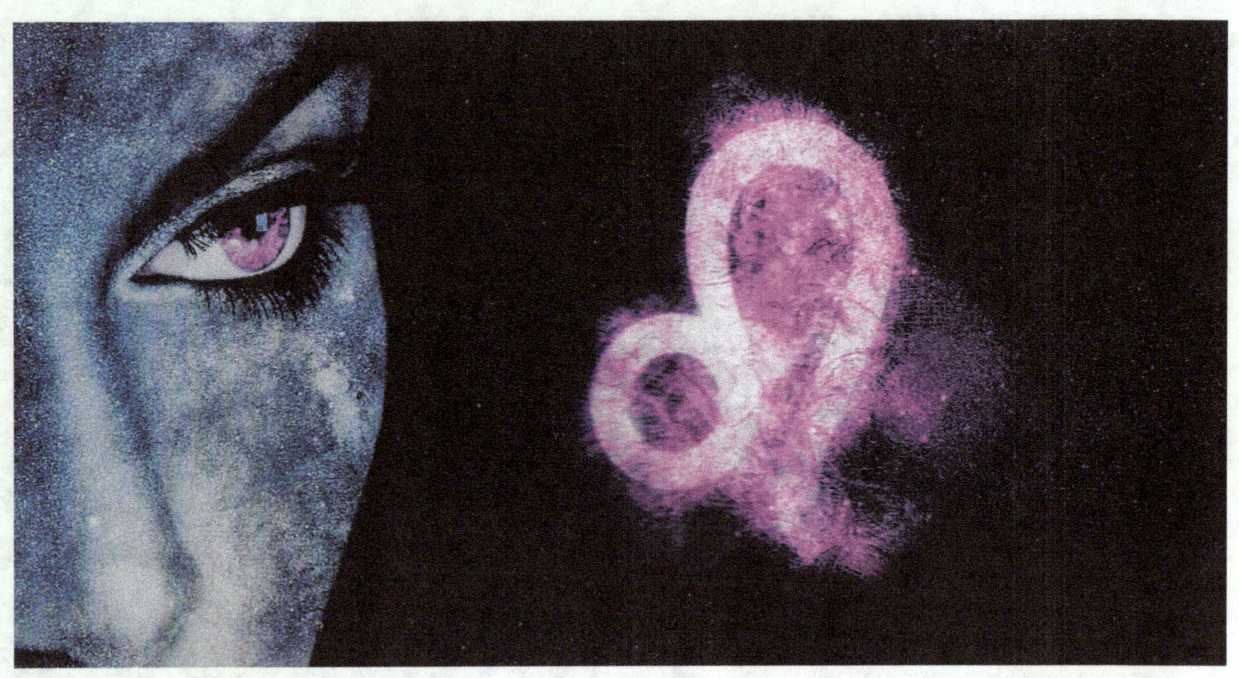

Happy Birthday LEO: 07/23 - 08/22

Fire symbol: Lion

Mind concerns: Action before thinking.

Body concerns: Heart, upper-back, sides.

Spiritual concerns: All that glitters is not gold! Jumping before researching can be trying.

Leo's are; flamboyant, love getting compliments, working, showbiz.

Topaz: Heart Chakra; May create good direction allowing Leo's to adjust and become centered the corrections is with the hard return allowing - Leo's. Keep in mind this is a reference guide and you want to view this book answers easy to find. Leo's to adjust and become centered.

Onyx: All Chakras: Planning your career? Using Onyx stone may calm this over worked taxed mind.

Sunstone: Sacral Chakra: Works well with Leo's, as this Gem represents the sun that is Leo's planet.

Herb: Ho-Shou-Wu: Chinese herb may be recommended nourish the blood brings elasticity promotes oxygen for the body aids in arthritis as it may strengthen the heart. It is part of the buckwheat family grown wild in China.

Virgo: Your ruler is Mercury. Color is Gray and Brownish at all times. Quick Silver is the solid and represents both female and male energy. this vibration is slightly picking up a bit more male energy, make no mistake this planet is self-contained, Mercury is a gather of information; it represents intelligence of knowledge a head and winged cap figure of Mercury, God and Goddess of commerce and communication, surmounting his caduceus staff. Mercury is the closest planet to the Sun, temperatures reach 800 degrees Fahrenheit and 427 degrees Celsius.

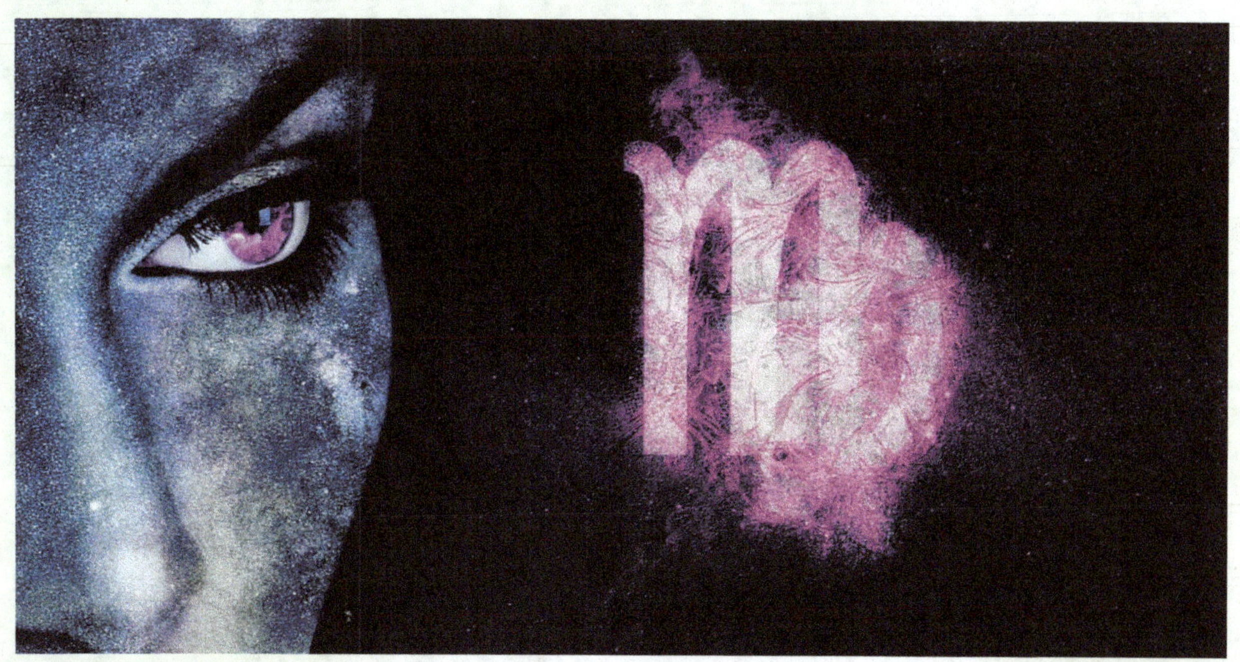

Happy Birthday VIRGO: 08/23 - 09/22.

Earth. symbol: Virgin.

Mind concerns: Active Mind.

Body concerns: Intestines, pancreas, gallbladder, and liver.

Spiritual concerns: You can't pour from an empty cup, take care of yourself first. If you don't invest in yourself first will others?

Virgo's are; Hard working, they remember everything, faithful, loving, artists,

Sapphire: Third Eye Chakra May bring clarity to your scope; May heal the nervous system, and regulate the thyroid giving strength to Virgo.

Tiger eye: Solar plexus Chakra: May tape stone to navel overnight. May be great for all chest and bronchial weaknesses may relieve headaches, depression. Tiger eye brings about leadership qualities for this Virgo's needs.

Jasper: Root Chakra: Provides mental balance for Virgo.

Herb: Passion flower may calm the nerves, an anti-inflammatory. May decrease insomnia, alcoholism. May eat the fruit and or make a tea from the dry leaf's and steam, may be sold in herbal stores. Shallow-rooted vine Various species grow throughout the tropics widely known to populate the Southern parts of the United States.

Libra: Your ruler is Venus. Color is pale Yellow. Copper is its solid and represents female energy. Symbols that represent Venus are, order, romance, money, partnership and equality. Venus is a force of love. Planet Venus is the Goddess of love and life, it is the second from the Sun, temperatures hit an all-time high from other plants of 870 degrees Fahrenheit and 427 degrees Celsius.

Happy Birthday LIBRA: 09/23 - 10/22.

Air. symbol: Balance of scales.

Mind concerns: Fitting in. Acceptance.

Body concerns: Kidney, lower back.

Spiritual concerns: It is a fine line between having substance and being aloof. Chop wood Carrie water.

Libra's are; diplomatic, overthinking, love fine items, shallow, ambitious.

Smoky quartz: Naval Chakra: May free ones self from harsh concerns, brings, about a new path, may relieve depression, and anxiousness.

Jade: Heart Chakra: Strengthen the mind and body.

Damiana: May be a wonderful hormone balancer for both mind and body men and women, may calm and subdue inflammation in the Kidneys. Grows on the hillside in brushy and scrub areas Southern California, Mexico, and South America quite reliably.

Chaparral

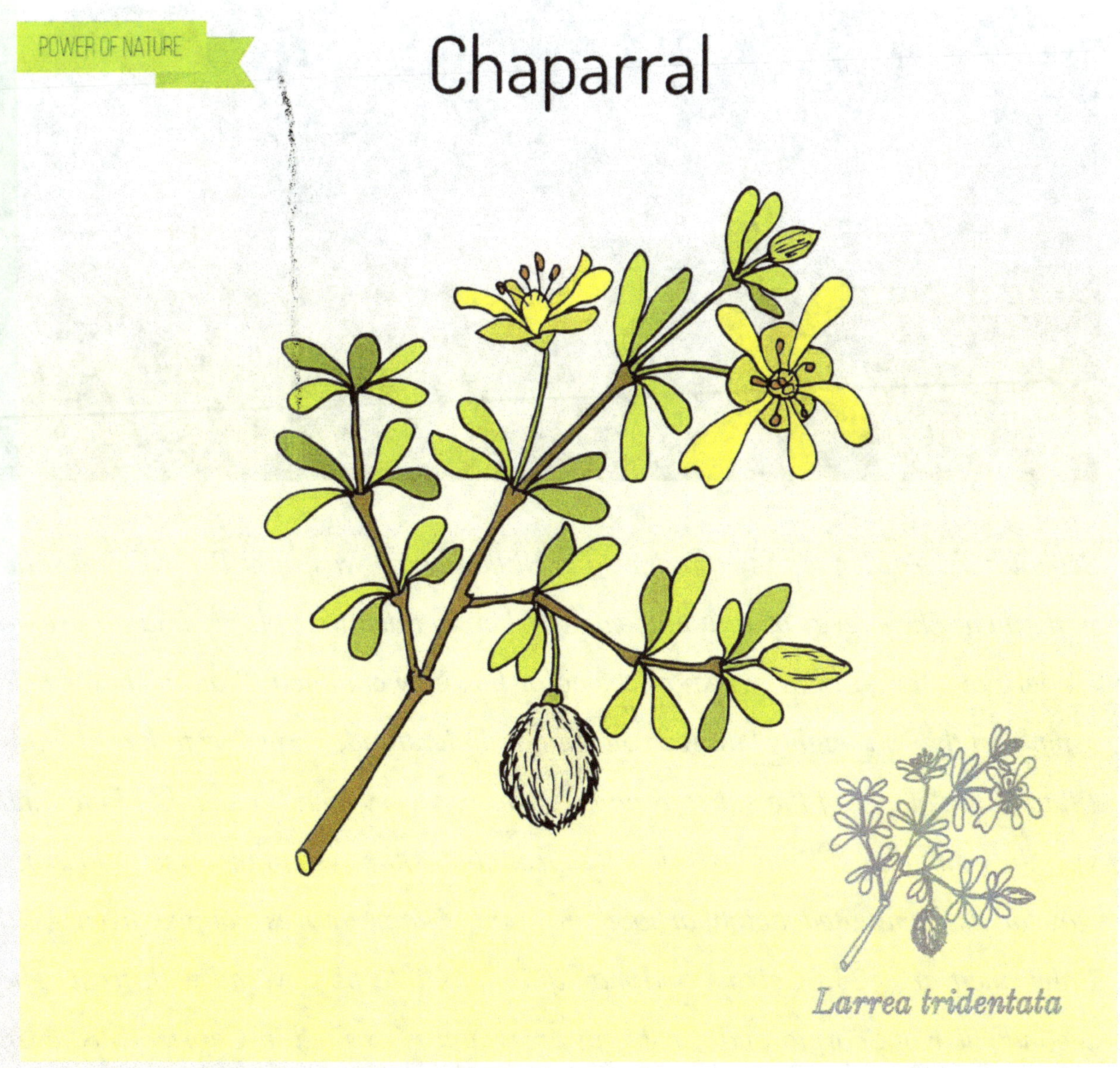

Chaparral: May dissolve tumors and cancers in the stomach, gallbladder and kidneys, urinary tract infection, also the upper repertory tract. Chaparral is found in the region of the Mediterranean Clements.

Scorpio: Your ruler is of two planets (1) Pluto. Color was light Brown. and solid plutonium. The energy of Pluto is female, when in this atmosphere. Images are no longer noted by N.A.S.A. we know the color has now changed. Pluto is the intense symbol of the "all mighty" things you cannot understand; known as father of Gods Pluto is the planet of the subconscious. Pluto is a very small and cold planet and was the ninth planet Pluto was demoted from the solar system because it does not stay in its dominated neighborhood in 2006. Temperatures ranged from -370 Fahrenheit and -233 Celsius and may quite possible be covered with frost. The second ruler of Scorpio and it rules in Aries and is exalted in Capricornus, even tho cap; is in Saturn. (2) Mars, color is Reddish Brown. Iron is the solid. and represents the male energy but because of the two planets only when the dominating mother allows. these duels planets make for assured self-containment. Mars has volcanoes due to the thin atmosphere known as God of war, Mars can't keep heat on average the planet is minus 80 degrees Fahrenheit and minus 60 Celsius.

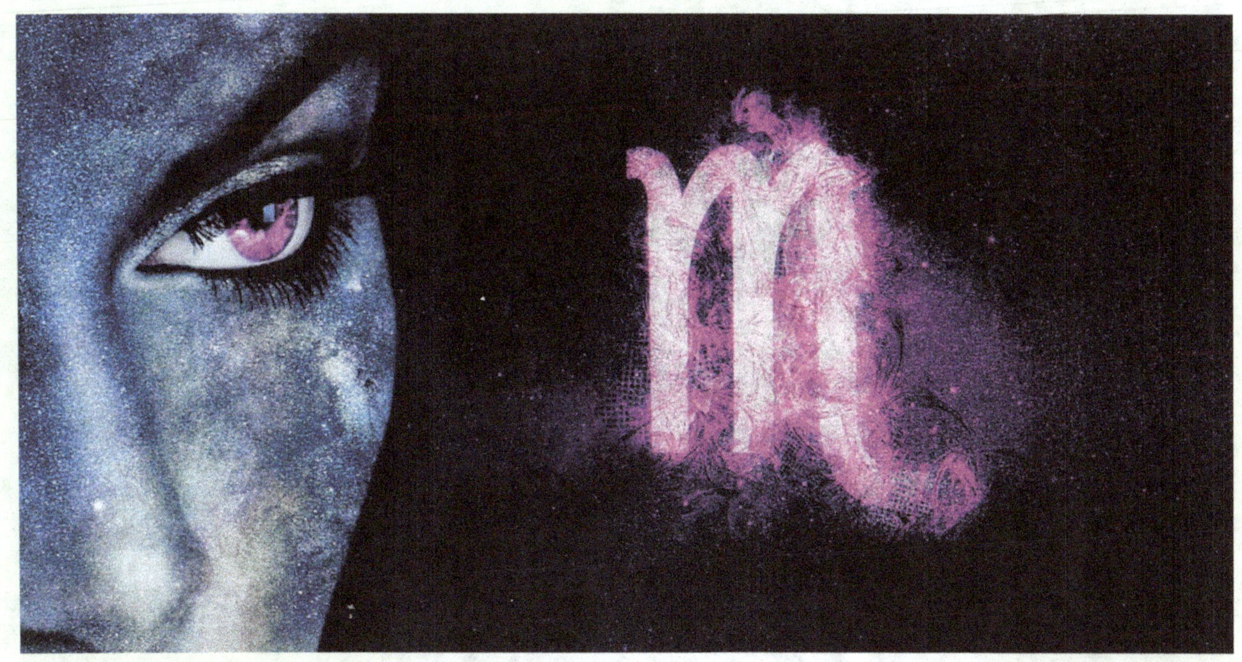

Happy Birthday SCORPIO: 10/23 - 11/22.

Water. symbol: Scorpion.

Mind concerns: Strategies, Precise planning.

Body concerns: Reproductive system, Genitals, Rectum, Bladder.

Spiritual concerns: Allowing other to aid in the ground work that your energy might be available for the project at hand;

A stitch in time saves nine.

Scorpio's are; passionate forming a cult, fearless, strategic, loving.

Hematite: Heart and root Chakra: May Prevent self-centeredness to this overly strong opinionated Scorpio balance by pulling out all the beauty, patience and peace to you and yours, (don't wet this stone).

Coral: Root Chakra: May protect you from ill feeling people namely jealously, may aid in restoring flow and function of the Genitals, Rectum and bladder.

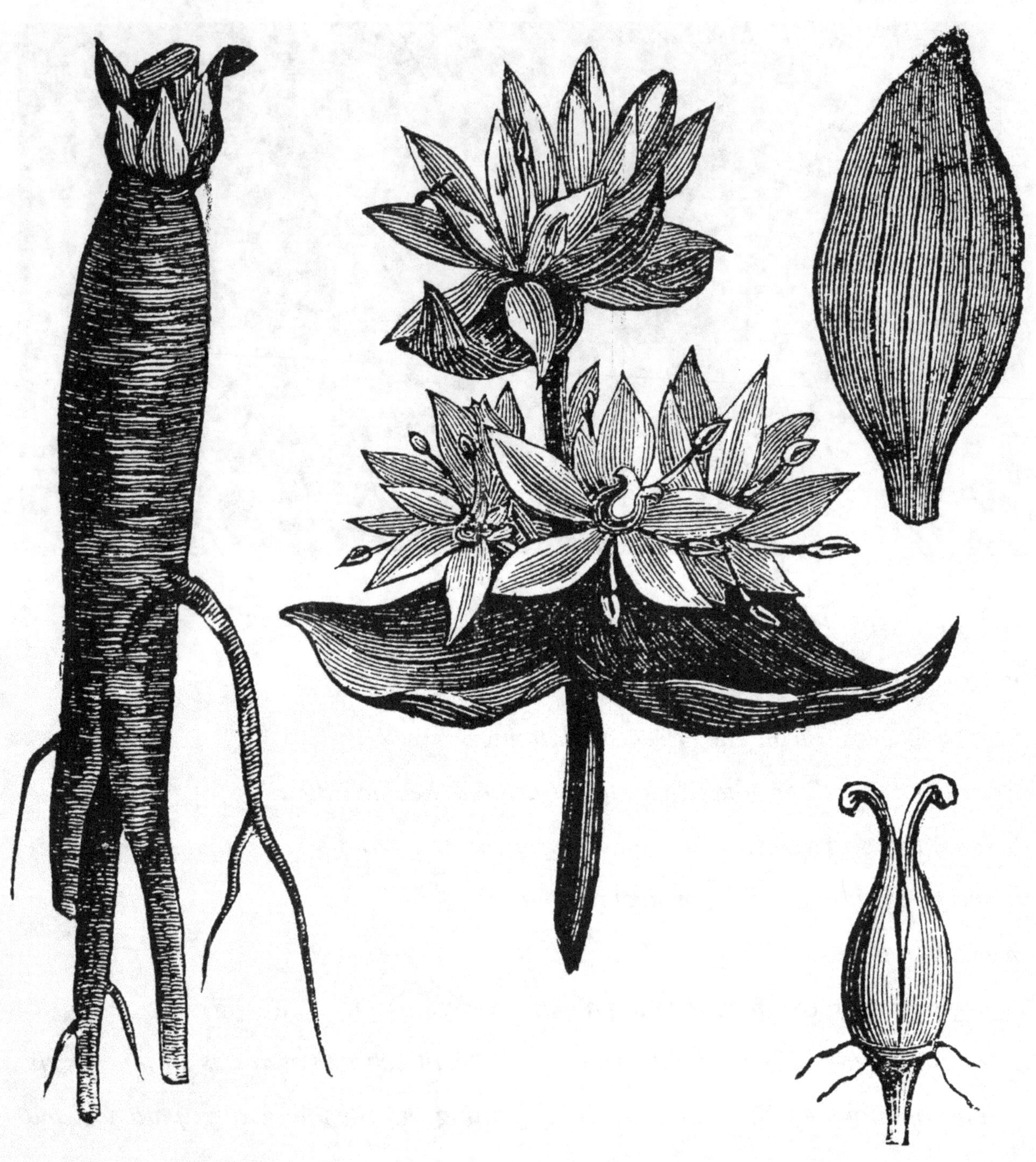

Herb: Siberian Ginseng: May aid in many nervous disorders due to mental stresses, may aid in circulating the fluid of the pituitary gland and prostate. can be found growing in thickets and in bunches in the cool forest area in China and Russia.

41

Sagittarius; Your ruler is Jupiter. Color is orange and has white bands, its solid is Tin. The energy represented here is male. Jupiter symbolizes God of the sky Zeus, heroic action, good luck in fortune exploration, and is the largest planet also the stormiest and runs second to Venus as to its bright shining value, but it is a close race. it is the fifth from the Sun, although the temperature is minus 145 degrees Celsius and minus 234 degrees Fahrenheit in the center of Jupiter is unequivocally hotter than the sun surface.

Happy Birthday Sagittarius: 11/23 - 12/21.

Fire. symbol: Archer on Horseback.

Mind concerns: Fixated on career, impulsive.

Body concerns: Upper-legs, Thigh, Hips.

Spiritual concerns: Invest in your dreams; Grind now play later, for the pay off Sagittarius are; Travelers, freedom to roam, honest, creates adventure, family.

Turquoise: Throat Chakra: May be an all-around healer may reduce inflammation, quicken the recovery of injury and or illness.

Lapis: Sixth, fifth Chakra: May cool the body temperature so; If you are the cool body type, take note of this (exercise) seek energy flow, otherwise it creates long term partnership and friends of true heart.

Obsidian: Root, all Chakra: May be a career finder a stable path, creating an even flow to life.

Herb: Oat straw may calm the nervousness, calm the nervousness, insomnia. May be a Heart strengthener, known to help mend broken bones due to its high calcium properties and a bladder corrector. Oat straw is Harvested in Washington State.

SATURN

Capricorn: Your ruler is Saturn. Color is pale Gold and in winters it changes to a pale Blue. its solid is lead. the energy represented here is male. The planets system symbolizes boundaries and limits. God of time. It is the only planet that has rings of ice, dust from its own shedding and orbiting rock around it all at the same time. It holds at least three orbiting rings in its simultaneous equations. Saturn is the sixth planet from the Sun and holds an average temperature of minus 288 degrees Fahrenheit and minus 177 degrees Celsius.

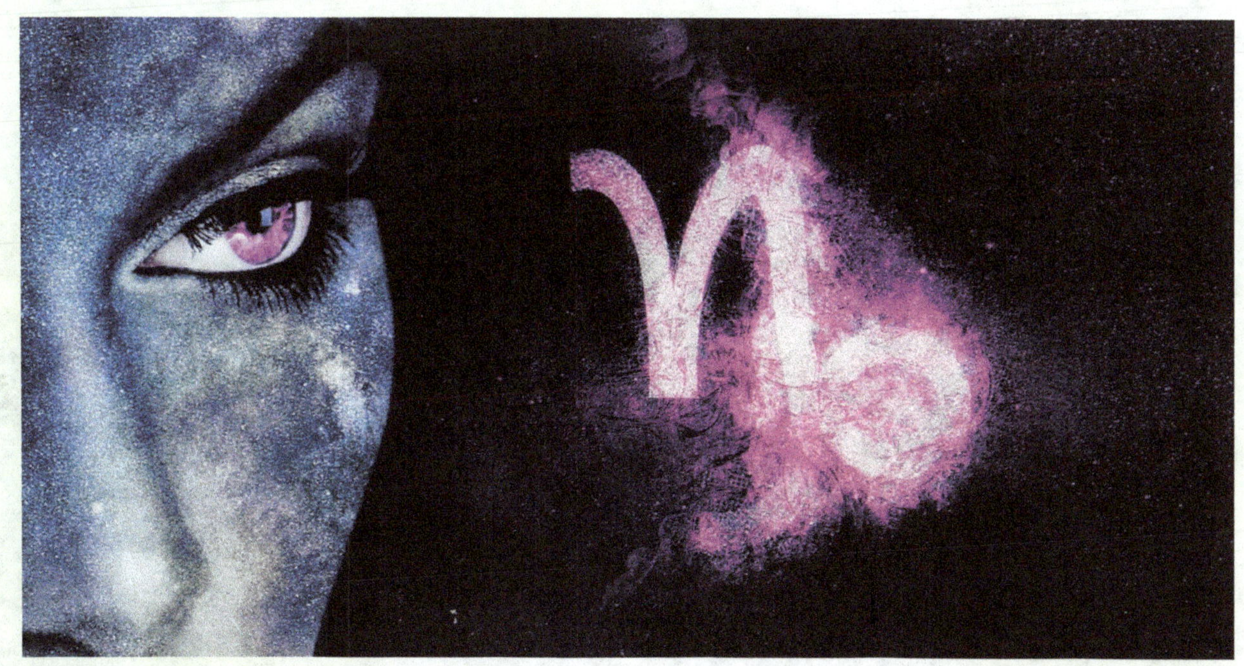

Happy Birthday CAPRICORN: 12/22 - 01/19

Earth sign: symbol: Goatfish.

Mind concerns: Stimulating to strengthen career direction, have a little more patients; Take it slow sometimes; Ask just don't do.

Body concerns: Knees, and, lower legs.

Spiritual concerns: Once bit twice shy; Wards off conflicts that no longer serves you, learned right!

Capricorns are; self-driven, persistent, realistic, sensitive, practical.

Garnet: Root Chakra: Aids circulation of the blood and strengthen the heart: Stimulates the memory, wards off evil souls and creates a joyful outlook.

Onyx: Root Chakra: A career builder and goal setter. This stone is filled with wisdom and grace, it may sense conflict and warns this Capricorn. The longer period of time that you wear it the more in tune you become.

Moss agate: Heart Chakra: Supports the detachment from things of time. May alleviate bad habits, addictions, clean and calm the kidney, lymph and digestion, and strengthens immune system.

Herb: Guggul: An anti-inflammatory, anti-rheumatic, - hinder arthritis pain. This tree is widely used in Ayurveda practitioners for centuries because its anti-inflammatory values and aids in weight loss it marries well with this Capricorn do to leg swelling, and circulation for the blood stream. commonly grown in India.

Aquarius's Ruler is two planets Uranus/Saturn. Color is pale Blue. Its solid is zinc. Both male and female are represented here in Uranus but the vibration is masculine, it is the seventh planet from the Sun. Uranus is said to be the oldest of the God's and symbolizes freedom, traits of being a revolutionary that visualizes new possibilities. This planet is the coldest in the solar system, at frigid levels temperatures minus 243 degrees Fahrenheit and 153 degrees Celsius, because it is made from ice rather than gas. Second Ruler is Saturn. Color is pale Gold and in winters it changes to a pale Blue. Its solid is lead. The energy represented here is male. The planets system symbolizes boundaries and limits. It is the only planet that has rings of ice, dust from its own shedding and orbiting rock around it all at the same time. It holds at least three orbiting rings in its simultaneous equations. Saturn is the sixth planet from the Sun, and its symbols is the Eagle, God of the seed sowing, and father Time. Powerful Saturn is referring to as Father of many Gods and was the original ruler of Aquarius. This planet holds an average temperature of minus 288 degrees Fahrenheit and minus 177 degrees Celsius.

Happy Birthday AQUARIUS: 01/20 - 02/19.

Air sign: symbol. A figure pouring oxygen into water.

Mind concerns: Revisiting your thoughts; Finding your personal direction.

Body concerns: Ankles, circulatory system.

Spiritual concerns: Freeing one's self, freedom from stigma. getting balance of self and relationships. Enjoy, Be childlike not childish.

Aquarius are; A helper to others, fun, fighting causes, shy, energetic.

Aquamarine: Fifth Chakra: It is used to obtain freedom in narrowing situations. Brings about unity in family and in business.

Jade: Sixth and solar plexus Chakra: May adhere this Aquarius to stick to the task at hand. Jade creates 5 wonderful attributes: compassion, courage, modesty, justice and wisdom.

Turquoise: Fifth Chakra: Turn your mind for partnership;
Tames the indifference between you and your partner.

Herb: Gentian: May be a blood-builder, and a stomach tonic. You may find that it aid in digestion, also strengthens the whole circulation system; But not used for heartburn as once used as it primary use. It has an anti-fungal and antibacterial treatment to it and are found in California, growing in rocky mountain areas and used in edible rock gardens; Gentian has many varieties.

Pisces: Your ruler is Neptune. The solid represented is Platinum. The color is pale blue and appears a little darker than Uranus and is a female energy. It is the eight planets from the Sun. Symbolizes the God of the sea and of many moons, brother of Jupiter and Pluto, Using the mighty trident Neptune is the intense intuitive, teacher of spiritual levels of subconscious dreams, illusions, fantasies, being a feminine energy, yet there are many layers you will find male influence here, deep feeling lead to compassion or strict discipline. this planet lacks a solid surface; The gas seeps down into the watery planet making slushy ice and water layers. Because of the wild weather Temperature can range 10 degrees up and down on each level minus 353 Fahrenheit and minus 214 Celsius.

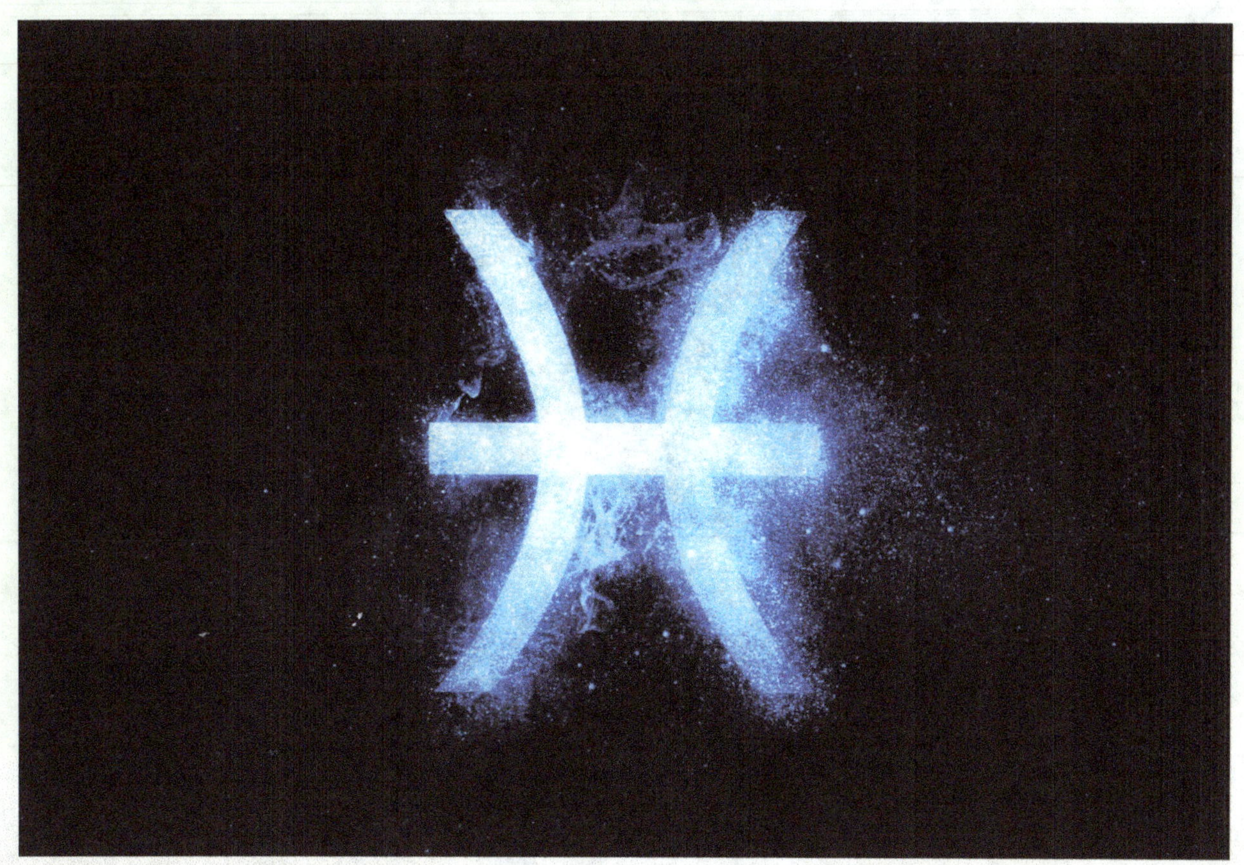

Happy Birthday PISCES: 02/20 - 03/20.

Water. symbol: Two fish swimming in circle.

Mind concerns: Love.

Body concerns: Feet.

Spiritual concerns: Both aspects are indicated here; Dreams that need to be put into action because faith without action is dead, time to get productive. Poor planning on others part is not an emergency on your part. Are you over extending?

Pisces are; Generous, amiable, positive, compassionate,

Amethyst: Sixth Chakra: Wellness and love is indicated for this Pisces expressing feelings; also, a money caller.

Jade: Sixth also solar plexus Chakra: brings love, harmony, wisdom, and trust.

Rose Quartz: Heart forth Chakra: May promote healing for heart, inner harmony; opens new paths.

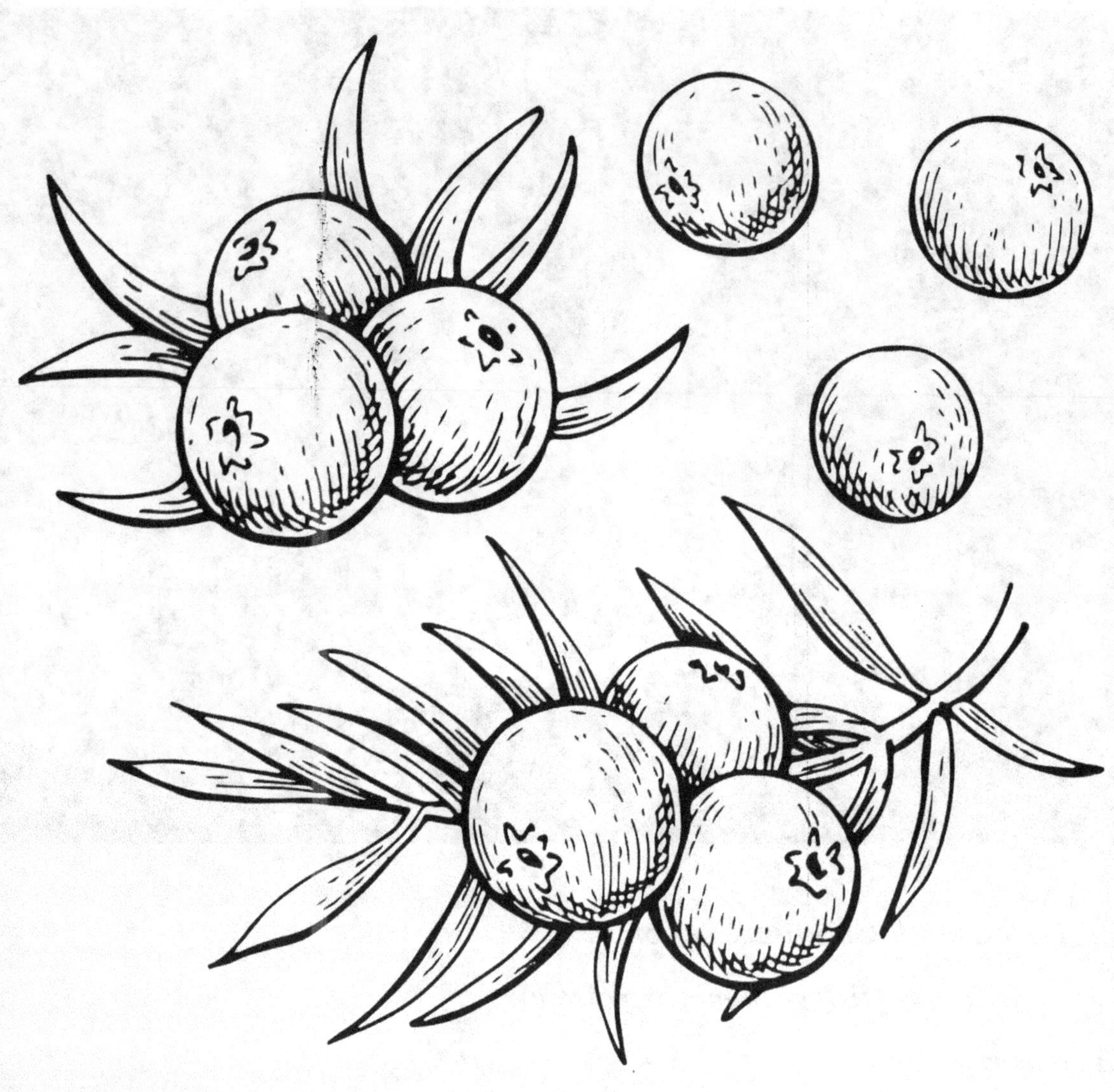

JUNIPER
HAND DRAWN
• *illustration* •

Herb: Juniper: The berries may improve digestion. If taken too long or in high doses may overly stimulate the kidneys. Drinking Coffee and alcohol may over stimulate.

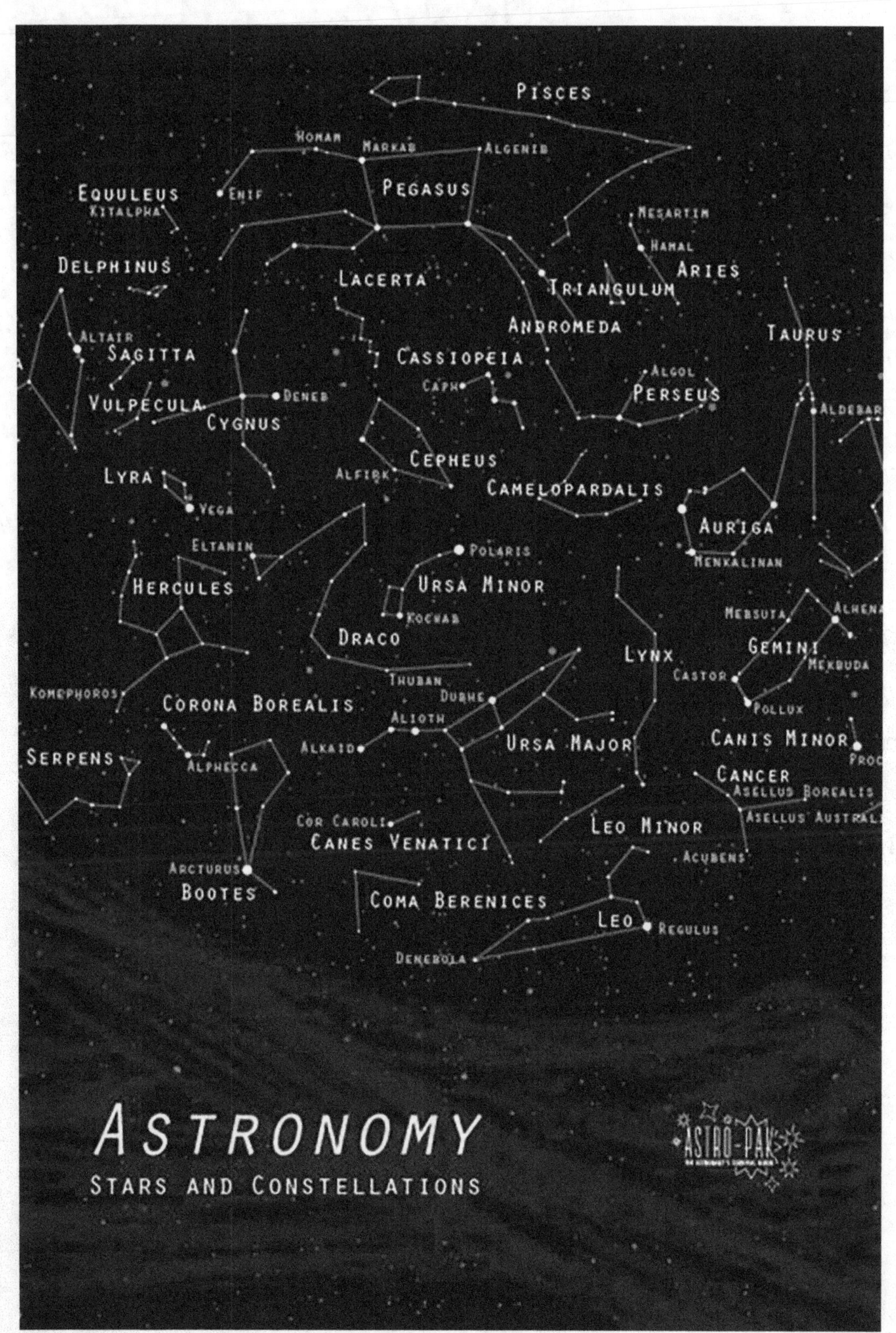

PISCES
HOMAM
MARKAB
ALGENIB
EQUULEUS
KITALPHA
ENIF
PEGASUS
MESARTIM
HAMAL
DELPHINUS
LACERTA
TRIANGULUM
ARIES
ANDROMEDA
TAURUS
ALTAIR
SAGITTA
CASSIOPEIA
CAPH
ALGOL
PERSEUS
ALDEBARAN
VULPECULA
DENEB
CYGNUS
CEPHEUS
LYRA
ALFIRK
CAMELOPARDALIS
AURIGA
VEGA
MENKALINAN
ELTANIN
POLARIS
MEBSUTA
ALHENA
HERCULES
URSA MINOR
GEMINI
KOCHAB
MEKBUDA
DRACO
LYNX
CASTOR
THUBAN
DUBHE
POLLUX
KOMEPHOROS
CORONA BOREALIS
ALIOTH
CANIS MINOR
SERPENS
ALKAID
URSA MAJOR
PROCYON
ALPHECCA
CANCER
ASELLUS BOREALIS
COR CAROLI
ASELLUS AUSTRALIS
CANES VENATICI
LEO MINOR
ACUBENS
ARCTURUS
BOOTES
COMA BERENICES
LEO
REGULUS
DENEBOLA

ASTRONOMY
STARS AND CONSTELLATIONS

ASTRO-PAK

CHAKRAS:

For thousands of years, information had been provided concerning the level of energy flow, and blockage pertaining to pressure points, in a word Chakras, places of the body that blood cells form liquid, for digestive functions.

Circulatory system influences the ears, eyes, and throat;

You have all of these energy fields located within your body.

The key, is to find your lower points and start building from there before you understand it, you have built a better you.

Best result has been made when you use the stones overnight and others first thing upon awaking.

As you can find in this coverage each rock has its own purpose. Find the ones that strengthen, calm, and create. use this book as are reference guide for different recipes for different times in your life.

By: Wendy Irwin
For sales and distribution
copyright@2009

Through the earths energy we can we can pick-up sound waves a song that relates to caves and mines individually right now are low ranges of 3-30 Hz of the electromagnet called by many "frequencies of the angles: or "problem solving" a cavity could pick up a 7Hz.

John 1:33 He upon whom you see the spirit descending and remaining upon Him, this is the One who baptizes in the Holy Spirit; Baptism in the Holy Spirit, The Holy Spirit (Greek word Pneuma) in the Gospel of John corresponds to the Praha of the Indian tradition.

Concerning the testimony of Saint John, the Baptist and the root charka calling it, with sound creating a frequency that you may form the sound with your mouth = UT Queant Laxis.

Ut, Re, Mi, Fa, Sol, Laxis a musical scale of sound Ut quant taxis resonate fibers Mira gesture family quorum, solve pollute labs reatum, Sancta Joannes.

St John the Baptist tells us how to release sin by using our own lips to utter the sounds, in order that your servant may be able to relate your request uttering sound to restore our birth right this merit restores authority and command magnum opus.

CHAKRA CHART:

(1) Root (RED) this Chakra is located in the middle of the genitals and rectum area it is an earth based absorbing Chakra and concerns it self with formulating teeth, nails, bone's, blood cells, intestines, prostate, and the spinal column. The gemstones that are effective here for each of the zodiac signs are Garnet, onyx, red jasper, picture jasper, diamond, rock crystal, ruby, coral, hematite and obsidian.

(2) Sacral (ORANGE) This Chakra is located above the pubic hair line, it is a water flowing Chakra and it concerns it's self with circulating fluids sweat, tears, urine, sperm, ovulation, and blood. This Chakra is all about the emotions of relationship with ones self and others the gemstones that are effective for harmonizing emotions are linked to each zodiac sign, the diamond, orange sapphire, rock crystal, black moonstone, peach moon stone, moon stone, onyx, sunstone, and obsidian.

(3) Solar Plexus (YELLOW) This is the belly button Chakra and it is a fire dwelling Chakra it is the alert system concerning itself with the bodies nervous system, stomach digestive, gall bladder and liver. It is all about mental alertness the gemstones that are effective here for each of the zodiac signs are; Jade, yellow jasper, leopard jasper, picture jasper, diamond, rock crystal, amber, tiger eye, smoky quartz, and obsidian.

(4) Heart This Chakra has three different values and colors, the Heart Chakra is located between and above your two breasts starting at the bottom of the heart Dark green. In the middle of the Chakra the color is Lime green The top of this Chakra is a Rosy pink. The heart concerns it self with circulating, pumping blood and fortifies the immune system. It is all about the three cycles of love. Dark green

or (1) hunter green, you no longer hunt, all your needs that you require are being hunted for, It is a wonderful thing to have what you deserve come to you, a harmonizing quality. The gemstones that are effective here for each of the zodiac signs are. Garnet, jade, diamond, aventurine, rock crystal, emerald, ruby, onyx, and obsidian, the second stage or value is (2) lime green, this heart Chakra is all about figuring out your heart's needs, what you want! and what you don't want! The hearts wants what it wants a spontaneous love on the move looking and searching for needs met. The gemstones that are effective here for each of the zodiac signs are Moss agate, rock crystal, topaz, onyx, light jade, hematite, and obsidian.

The top of the heart Chakra is the color Rosy pink or pink champagne bubbling with enthusiasm. This can be puppy love, or the beginning stages of attraction to love. A pure love gentle, open, vulnerable, and invites unconditional love; The gemstones that are effective here for each of the zodiac signs are; Rose quartz, rhodochrosite, diamond, rock crystal, pink ruby, onyx, pink jade, pink coral, and obsidian.

(5) Throat (BLUE & GREEN) This Chakra is located at the base of the neck it is the air in your cavity it concerns it self with the thyroid gland, ears, eyes, nose, and throat functions. It is all about the breath, ether, because it is the communicator. This can spill over into the thymus Chakra that it is located between the heart and throat, where it can strengthened The thymus when activated. The gemstones that are effective here for each of the zodiac signs are Moss agate, aquamarine, blue sapphire, turquoise, diamond, rock crystal, topaz, onyx, smoky quartz, lapis, and obsidian.

(6) Third Eye (BLUE & PURPLE) located on the forehead. This Chakra concerns itself with understanding, intuitive thinking, perception. It is all about your inner

knowledge, the change you bring about when growing your intuitive sight. The gemstones that are effective here for each of the zodiac sign are; Silver, diamond, blue sapphire, amethyst, aquamarine, onyx, jade, turquoise, lapis, and obsidian.

(7) Crown (VIOLET, WHITE & GOLD, This Chakra is located on top of your head and it concerns are developing and processing high levels of energy, for new thinking for enlightenment from spirit to soul, all vibrations have been gathered here and it never dies, because it is pure energy, so treat it like gold because you are. We will live as kings and queens but will die like men, in other words, we manifest into this vessel for earthly missions and transmute back to source space and time light and dust. The gemstones that are effective here for each of the zodiac signs are; Gold, diamond, amethyst, purple jade, aquamarine, aventurine, blue sapphire, rock crystal, moon stone, onyx, lapis, and obsidian.

Restore; Renew; Revitalize;

Reaping the benefits from your little Gem's!

Restoring = brings back the luster of the healing mission your rock carries.

Renewing = after you have discovered the healing properties your gem has released and you will see the appearance is different as a dull or cloudy mark or haze is presence you may find these tips renew the life of your rock!

Revitalizing = now you have completed, new life by refreshing the vitality, for your rock now setting your intention, for your mission into the rocks and place on the desired Chakra.

Let's Rock and Roll!

Talk to them! That they shall feel your words!

Carefully as your wish is their mission;

You may start out, by a short thought, I am happiest when,

I am ———.

example = loving, well received, harmonious.

See nothing is asked for, and nothing is something when you're not in a state of I want, or I need, it only reinforces things you do not have.

You may clean your gems in warm running water, and prep them with a little pat, from one of the following: Holy water; White rum; Rubbing alcohol, or Salt water, and setting your intention. by placing them in the Sun light or Moon light. I am delighted to see you working at full value, and give them a smile, Seeking out your gemstones as your preference them.

I enjoy this, I enjoy that, example: I prefer you to absorb pure **love**. I prefer you to **accept** helpings of abundance, I prefer you my wonderful little well and vibrant gem.

yearning, grasping, needed for prayer answered= See how this vibration is not a place of openness or oneness with head and heart it is countering your intention even blocking you roads because the intention equals conflict Replace it now with I prefer you when you are absorbing good health; Healthy mind set healthy heart. see how this just covered Love, Money, Health.
words of wisdom, a word to the brilliant, do not use it for bad, it will come at you, and with three-fold, the best revenge is higher ground. Best Blessing Wendy in-so-much.

Amethysts: *Healing attributes; Problem solver, proactive of owner, wards off robbers. Amethysts is a calming gem that balances mood swings connotes fear, rage, sadness, and grief, as continual use it promotes psychic abilities, soothes the mind for a calm night sleep, used in meditation, and in large stones of two feet and higher a catch all, as visitors enter the house; Because it is a gem of purity, spiritual insight may be achieved for clear third eye visionaries.*

History; of Amethyst; *Vikings used it to look through when viewing the sun to navigate their ship ventures by sea.*

According to Greek mythology; *Amethyst was a virgin, and was fix-sated on by the Greek God Dionysus after drinking red wine, being in his state of intoxication, Amethyst, called out to Goddess Diana for help, who intern, cast the virgin into a white shimmering stone, known today as Quartz.*

Aquamarine; Healing Attributes; *A handy gem for safe travel, builds courage in communication, calms the pollutants, in and around thy dwelling, concerning any conflicts; The stone also relates to suppressed memories, trauma, that needs emotional healing, it clears the mind and calms the heart.*

History: of Aquamarine; *First discovered in Siberian 1723. When magma under the earth crust interacts with mineral rich rocks called pegmatites, when high levels of heat buildup, it forms pegmatites, most aquamarine are then formed, and can be found in mountains worldwide to date.*

According to Greek mythology: *Aquamarine, the gem came from a mermaids jewelry box, and that the gem will revile decrement, the egg that mama laid (mermaids marmalade) by changing color from light to dark when around friend of true heart. Greeks used the stone to carve the image of sea God Poseidon, to* *protect sailors, over stormy waters, also known as the sacred jewel of Neptune.*

Aventurine; *Healing Attributes; Conditioning the skin, clearing up many irritants, acne, dandruff, and used as an eye wash, clearing up dry skin, when the gem is placed in a container of water, and used as a body rinse in-turn soothes the skin.*

History: *Aventurine; Predominately found in China, Nepal, Tibet; and Europe. in the 18th century the Italians called it all adventure this meaning is, one by chances, if one came across it by chance, Green aventurine has been used as a healing stone for the lungs, heart, and sinuses.*

According to Greek mythology: *Aventurine was used to enhance good humor, lightheartedness, to brighten the day, also it was sewn into the Greeks solders clothes, as a special request for men, creating courage, when preparing for war. Coral; Healing attributes: wards off jealousy; For women it balances menopausal systems; For men it balances erectile glands, and as a bone strengthener, it enhances circulation, blood flow, forming of new tissue.*

History: *growing on rocky sea bottoms, also found in dark caverns mainly in the Mediterranean Sea.*

According to Greek mythology: *Coral was Greek God Perseus beheaded Gorgon Medusa the blood shed to the ocean forming a petrified rock shell, known to date as red coral.*

Diamond; Healing attributes: *A great recipe for alleviating stress, by drinking diamond water, first upon awaking, aids in mental confusion when placed on the third eye leads to opening the third eye.*

History: Diamond where Found nine hundred million year ago in China, and India, and also known to have surfaced in the 4th century BC.

According to Greek mythology: Diamonds; Adamas and Adamant where the sons of Cronus both conformed and execute the castration of Uranus with a Diamond sickle, that was than given to Gaia the boys mother.

Emerald; Healing Attributes: It has been a well-known practice to strengthen weak eyes by inserting micro bit of the emerald into the eye duct creating effective vision, and reducing head inflammations and developing mental growth. iinnerknowledge.

History: Emerald they are found in igneous, metamorphic, and sedimentary rocks all over the world; The three front runners for best quality are Brazil, Colombia, and Zambia.

According to Greek mythology: Mercury was said to favor the stone emerald, being the God of commerce, mercury made the emerald the God of travel. Venus Goddess of love and wealth, used the stone to see if her lovers are unfaithful, if the heart is loyal the gem would glow, but if the lover was untrue the gem became dull, and cloudy.

Garnet; Healing attributes: A strengthener of blood, memory, and heart, as it works as a reflectance turning away negative energy, dispelling evil souls.

History: Pyrope Garnets are found in Sri Lanka Thailand India. Spessartine in Kenya, Madagascar.

According to Greek mythology: The word Garnet came from the word pomegranate its meaning is, seed; Persephone Goddess of sunshine, when packing *for travel, Hades gave Persephone pomegranate seeds, "Garnet" ensuring her return, ancient Greeks highly valued the gem stone ring as they used it for sealing important documents.*

Jade; Healing attributes: *lower high tempters during cold and flu season, it detoxifies the body by stimulating the kidneys, so do a detox drink for optimal benefit, jade also will bring renewed thinking.*

History: *Jade; found in China, Egypt, and Mexico.*

According to Greek mythology: *Jade; Greek Goddess Moerae means the three parts of fate because, the roll is played out in 3 ways one determining a person's fate, or lot in life, determining the course of the child, three days after birth. this may be blunt, but this is their job, deciding peoples's path's, just by looking into the stone, the future is told who has what job. 1 is Moire = spinner, she spins the thread of life each on child born; 2 is Lakhesis = apportioned of lot's, measuring the thread of the child's life, she decides how much time a person shall live; 3 is Atropos = she who cannot be turned, her job is to cut the thread of life, to end a person's life. The goddess is also referred to as the three ugly hags, hard and ridged.*

Jasper; Healing Attributes; *a stone of courage and is connected to the earth, it is a gem of grounding and used for good understanding and stability, balances the yin and yang energy calling on both mother earth and father time.*

History: *According to Greek mythology: Jasper is linked to Greek Goddess Gaia and offered to her by Callisto Goddess of the moon.*

Hematite: Healing Attributes; *a protective gem concerning positive, and negative energy, it actually absorbs negative emotions of the wearer, and transforms them into positive energy. is not to be wet, but prep in a cup of loose rock crystal* *overnight, and or placed in the Moon light, absorbing female energy, and or Sun light to absorb male energy. it can be set for both absorbing energies depending on your intention.*

***History**; Hematite is found in Greece, and is often called ema, meaning blood, that is undesirably showed to be a brick red color, when the stone has beed lanced or the gem has been grounded into power.*

***According to Greek mythology;** Hematite is a gemstone Greeks often rubbed on the body to conduct one's self invincible in battle. Hematite is connected to the Greek God Aries Mars in the Roman path and both affiliates with the God of war.*

***Lapis; Healing Attributes;** Blue Lapis was used as a personal proctor, a stone of wisdom, and truth, when worn as a head band it ensures one's own perspective, and that it would be insured of a pure focused outcome, protecting this thought process, so that, in speech the direction given shall not go awry.*

***History:** Blue Lapis or in other words Lapis lazuli the blue of the deep sea and blue skies artists ground the gem to achieve the color of ultramarine; The Egyptians used it to make blue cosmetics; most popular mine found in the Kokcha river located in Afghanistan, and harvested it from the sat-e-sang mind for over 6,000 years.*

***According to Greek mythology:** Lapis lazuli; called by Greeks, the chosen ones; The diamond runs in second place of the Lapis; Not many in power where allowed to hold or take possession of the due to gem its high levels of powers known to create tsunamis, wild storms, and natural climate changes; The oracles and prophets, would use great discernment when choosing the Greek God to bear the gem, to insure that it would not be used for evil.*

Moonstone; *Healing, aiding in the reduction of anxiety nervous disorders, and hyper active individuals, although it encourages an open mind bringing in joy, it calms the mind for study and concentration.*

History: *Moonstone is Harvested and found in Sri Lanka, Brazil, for many centuries, the pebbles were woven into the bride's garment, use to attract the grooms romance on the wedding night; The large stones were brought into the house to create fertility for a large family.*

According to Greek mythology: *Goddess of love Aphrodite and Goddess of the moon, Selene her path is a woman riding side settle on a horse or driving a chariot on the lunar crescent, her greatest love was Endymion a shepherd prince Zeus granted him eternal youth and an immortal, but was put into slumber in a cove in Mount Latmos where Selene goes to him every night;*
The stone is widely sought after for ensured safety of night travelers

Moss Agate; Healing Attributes; *To change the luck of one's hardships most likely due to one's own thought process or over thinking or drinking, It has become the drinking, It has become the gem of gamblers said to be a true money caller, eliminating bad habits and triggers. drinking the water after soaking the gem overnight may stabilize one's kidneys, aiding in digestion.*

History: *found in chips and pieces from the volcanic after mass in India, Europe, and United States. Moss Agate is also called mocha stone, It is linked to the earth and harvest time, used in the crops to produce a grand gathering from the soil. Gardeners would put the gem in the garden to insure abundance.*

According to Greek mythology: *Moss Agate Mother Earth Gaia, known as Greek*

Goddess of the night sky, was one who governed the universe before the Titans took over, Goddess Gaia gave birth to Titans, Uranus, Primordial, God of the sea and also Pontus, who is a giant and God of the sea, also she came in the shape of Gaea creating mountains, plains, rivers, oceans; Greek Goddess Aurore. Uranus put a stop to Gaea from earthly creations, by putting a seal over her womb, enclosing the seedling in her, stopping the birth of any more children, causing her allegiance to her Titan son Cronus, using an iron sickle created by his mother was able to overthrew Uranus casting drop of his blood on earth becoming the spirit of punishment. (Erinyes)

Obsidian: Healing Attributes; A strong pain reliever as it brings good luck, blessing on what currently concerns you a master plan can be hatched with the use of Obsidian, it draws out negative poison from over thinking, it blocks spiritual attacks and stabilizes the owner path for healthy relationships, and wealth.

History: Obsidian was used as a weapon sharpen as a dagger, ax, or spear head, found in the volcanic after eruptions. The obsidian can produce rock fragments so sharp that when inflicted on the victim, he would often flee as the shards cut deep and in small hand to hand stabs where unbearable to continue the battle, to date black Obsidian is used for wrist watches due to its state-of-the-art stone of elegant, a true classic statement that safeguards the owner's good fortune.

According to Greek mythology: Obsidian: God of the underworld Hades, the name came from the adobe of the dead, as the God of wealth and prosper Hades also called Pluto the wealth one after Cronus was concurred by his son the kingdom was divided Hades fell and there he ruled with his Queen Persephone over the fire and over the dead, known as the house of Hades, Hades is the eldest male of Cronus and Rhea.

Onyx; Healing Attributes; *Creating stamina steadfast in decision making a confidence builder creating self-esteem and self-control a powerful stone in decrement and wisdom. As this gem Transforms negative energy to positive as it helps you to absorb personal strength.*

History: *The Egyptians carved their bowls out of the stone.*

According to Greek mythology: *Onyx; The Greeks called it the claw, because the light color stone can look like finger nail color, one day when Venus was sleeping Cupid her son, used the stone to trim his mother's finger nails, as legend has it the nails of a Goddess are unable to cut never-the-less Venus fingers nails transformed into onyx that day and this story is set in stone.*

Rhodochrosite; Healing Attributes; *is a gemstone that stimulates heart and head energy spiritual and physical, just looking at the stone is said to bring a smile to your face that warms your heart as it calms your emotions strengthening your heart supporting wellbeing.*

History: *Rhodochrosite is a pink and white vein mineral and carries a strong value of manganese first found in Roman in low temperatures known as the gem of self-love and compassion it moves one believe towards healing, The name of this gem comes from the Greek word rhodkhros or radon, that meaning is, a pink rose, you may find different shades of the gem from a bright pink cotton candy to a pink stripe like a candy cane in Spain, Africa, Peru, and the state of Montana you will may find the gem has black spots periodically on the gem. Because the stone it not very dense it is used in cosmetics for its mineral properties.*

According to Greek mythology: *Rhodochrosite; Nisaba Goddess of knowledge, writing, and wheat, she is the goddess of accounts of the Gods; Nisaba was first* known as the grain Goddess worshiped in the city, daughter of Anu and Unas from Sumerian, the balance of Heaven and earth,

Rose quartz; Healing Attributes; Rose Quartz has a huge benefit for dispelling radiation, you may place a chunk by your phone and computer while in use, wear a bracelet, and neckless, will work wonders as well. using the gem as a guide by placing the gem in water over night and drinking it, may bring one's awareness of true love, this gem is also used as a is also used as a fertility enhancer by string up the libido.

History: Rose quartz is found in Brazil, Madagascar, a gem of soft and gentleness of the heart, a true energy that aids with awkwardness, opening the heart to express fulfillment of one's true needs

According to Greek mythology: Cupid and Eros brought rose quartz, into recognition for the purpose of creating a spark of one's true desire of love. Aphrodite the Goddess of love, and lust, known for her beauty; Adonis who was Aphrodite's lover was hit from behind by Ares, when he took the form of a pig, Aphrodite came to the aid of Adonis, and in the hustle, she was cut and her blood mixed with Adonis paired together formed a white pink veined quartz, Zeus rescued Adonis and put the rose quarts in their dwelling to preserve this union, and is a symbol of true love to date.

Rudy; Healing Attributes; Heal the heart, liver, eyes, creates circulation for the genital, a blood cell builder, also known to be an ally to shield against plagues, also rubies are a gem, to be warn, to ward off infections, fever, and heart attacks.

History: Rubies are found in Siberia, Afghanistan, Pakistan, and used as money, ready made from the earth cash, as well as the Sapphires, emeralds, diamonds, silver and gold as the front runner of trade. Rudy's are said to be the most precious from the 12 gemstones created by God, the father maker of heaven, and earth and all that is seen and unseen.

According to Greek mythology: *Rubies; Plutus is the Greek god of wealth and fire, son of Demeter the Goddess of harvest, and fertility; and of lesion a hero, from the island of Crete; Plutus was blinded as a young boy, when Zeus took away his sight, so that the wealth god would not only give to what was pleasing to the eye, but would hear the true cause, bestowing upon him, then he could chooses the measure of abundance of wealth, to give, this is the depiction we see today as a boy carrying a horn shaped basket, of wheat called a cornucopia.*

Sapphire; Healing Attributes; *reduces the flutter of a nervous heart, creates a value for friends of true heart, release spiritual confusion, calmed the mind attributes of spiritually to see beyond surface knowledge, enhances a cheerful disposition and a joyful life.*

History: *In ancient times if sapphire where give to mortals for it magical powers, the gem would not shine for thus with evil intention or souls. In ancient Greece and Rome sapphires where warn only by kings and queens because of its royal color and said to have brought special insight for the mind to form a protection from two faced people. Sapphires found in the state of Montana in 1865 by gold prospectors and in Nepal, Sri Lanka, Pakistan over 150 million years ago, these gems formed in the earth over intense heat and pressure that is why the gems have such a high density. In Exodus says the second set of commandments said that the tablets or Talmud, given to mosses by God, was etched in blue sapphire, a symbol of heaven and earth and in turn making it the value of Gods throne.*

***According to Greek mythology:** Sapphire; Greek Gods believed the world was placed upon the blue rock; Prometheus is the Greek Goddess of the Blue glass; Another tale of Greek mythology is of Oceanids the water nymph's daughter of Titan Oceanus of 3000 sisters of the sea, being the mother of the sea daughters, she herself was half mermaid, and half marine flower; The father was the river God, and of oceans, as well as all fresh waters, and of all saltwater alike, encircling the entire world.*

***Smoky quarts; Healing Attributes;** Is said to lift the sorrows of the world, protecting soldiers at war, uplifting the moral to win the war, Smoky quarts balances the fluid in the joints to calm any inflation tempering arthritis, stiffness, and pain, as well as strengthening the fluid in the body for muscle endurance,*

***History:** Smoky quartz is the National gemstone of Scotland and can be traced back to the country as having the eldest association with the gems organ from 300 B.C. mined from the cairngorm mountains and made in to kilt pins, as a power stone, it was also made for war, as a sock knife or in other words a sgian dubh.*

***According to Greek mythology:** The meaning of the word smoky quartz; means "not drunken" as it protect one from the effects of alcohol, This is a path found of Persephone Goddess of spring, found and made a necklace of smoky quartz, to shed light on death and the afterlife, made of 12 beads and a loop departing by a large bead, the pendant is carved out of crystal in the shape of a skull, symbolizing safe passages; This neckless and or prayer beads are made to represent the Pomegranate Goddess also known as Persephone Goddess of sunshine, the path of Persephone Goddess of spring, is made as seed agreement, that the pomegranate seed has been eaten a symbol of safe travels. releasing negative thinking and conflict the gem absorbs sorrow, and to be thrown back into the earth for healing,*

Hecate Greek Goddess of wisdom, crossroads, ghosts, and the dark moon, secrets of heavens and earth as well as the underworld who honors Goddess Gaia and Goddess Persephone.

Tiger eye; Healing Attributes; *Filled with leadership authority and grace, releasing inflammation in the head creating a relax state for commanding positions, also restores the lungs from insecurities aiding in breathing hindrances, strengthens one's gut, that you keep your eyes focused on the task at hand, trusting your insight.*

History: *Thousands of years ago Tiger eye was carved into special talismans to cure whatever the cause happened to be, the golden-brown quartz was used as a signature gem in accordance with many different recipes and in many different cultures worldwide, Tiger eye is one of the most valuable gems in the trade market to date, sawed after because of it beautiful it holds a very high dollar amount, a cut stone has a been known to have sold for $5,000 dollars.*

According to Greek mythology: *Persephone the Greek Goddess of spring and is closely linked to planet Mercury, had used the tiger eye against the evil eye and curses of bad luck as the stone has great power in combat, Athena Greek Goddess of wisdom, and justice, she used it as a protector, from unwise paths. Apollo Greek God of music had been said to wear a bracelet of tiger eye that was a band, he used for prayer, calling on health and healing.*

Topaz: Healing Attributes; *This gem brings motivation, to any mind set, stimulating your world, working to create energy flow, the focus is on truth, and harmony, bringing good luck, and blessing to a joyful heart. Using the blue topaz Stimulates communication, and calms a nervous throat.*

History: *in Russia pink topaz was harvested and used for a love stone, warming the hearts of the owners, this stone was so brilliant at one time, it caught the eye of the royal families, in the 19th century the royal family "czar" kept the gem way from general population for quite some time; the Greek word for topaz is topaz-ion as this word is taken from the meaning of fire, and sanskrit.*

According to Greek mythology: *As a direct line to Jupiter the gem topaz was used by its wearer, Topaz to become invisible to protect against disease, and untimely death; Egyptians called topaz the golden glow the sun god of Ra; Who is all so the God of the Sun also he honored Demeter Greek Goddess of abundance of the harvest.*

Turquoise: Healing Attributes; *The sleeping beauty turquoise is a very bright blue and it almost looks like plastic gemstone it is used for clearing the vocal cords and calming the air or either in the tube area; lime green turquoise is a healer for the heart and thymus, creating a call for things you want and things you grow out of; Spiny oyster shell turquoise, given its name by native Americans and out of the gulf of Mexico has an 4 colored stones all conglomerated together, bright orange, yellow, light blue, white, and a black fine threat going through it used to bring out the joy in life,*
Dark green turquoise is used to heal accumulated stress by calming the owners mind, body, and nervous system gradually so it a good gem to wear so it a good gem to wear for periods of time, all turquoise heals but some are used for a finer pin point remade it dispels negative energy and prevents attacks, with in and out.

History: *An all-time favorite of the Chinese, mined in China caves for over 2,000. years, producing a beautiful color spectrum in America, the demand was so high that the gem became pricy; there about 1980's, after about 15 years stint, the best*

Chinese turquoise was mostly sold among quaint little shops, and circulated within the scope of the families and friends who wholesales and retailed the gem; Green or lime green turquoise most commonly has a copper vine running through it making the gem one to aid in circulation, although there are many stones names and healing properties from each variety; The dark blue with the traditional spider webbing could be from a very popular mine is the in China mine called Number & the Lander Blue. Most turquoise out of China are harvested out of the Hubei province and also out of Anhul, and the yungai, and the Zhuxi mines.

According to Greek mythology *one morning Greek Goddess Danae awoke to the sound of rainfall plink plink plink in her room as she opened her eyes to her surprise she saw golden glistening drops of water it made a distinct sound creating a talking pattern as she heard "Danae you are very rich now in wealth and beauty" Danae could barely believe her ears and eyes for she had blossomed into a beautiful young lady, her father was always a jealous man that kept Danae in a small room with only an old hag to talk to; Danae began to feel overjoyed as she rose up with laughter, finding her skirt wet with golden due, soon after that she saw Zeus; Suddenly Danae's only friend the old hag became a fair-skinned nanny, nine months later Danae gave birth to a son, all three lived together in a pod made of bronze, one day Danae's father Acrisius, heard a sound coming from the pod and found them.*

Acrisius killed the nanny, put Danae and her child into a chest carved of wood, and threw it into the sea, Zeus using his force of wind blew the box to a fisherman's cove, where a single man was fishing, Zeus put the floating chest in his sights, Danae and her son Perseus, and the single man, we're all so very glad to see each other, the single man took Danae as his wife and raise the boy as his own.

They lived a joyful life with a spring in their step and song in their heart. Later that year yachts were built by Danae's husband Dictys to spread the information about the herbal teas provided in Root's and Rock's, sharing ingredients to create Whimsical Recipes now available for all who yearn for a healthier joyful lifestyle.

as they christen the yacht in the name of the "YouTube" channel Healthy Recipes with Wisdom.

Enjoy your life and Best Blessing for you and yours Wendy.

iinnerKNOWLEDGE
my IK-SPA.com
for mind, body & sprit